Messner Holiday Library
Jewish Holiday Fun
by Judith Hoffman Corwin

Julian Messner

Copyright © 1987 by Judith Hoffman Corwin

Published by Julian Messner,
a division of Simon & Schuster,
Simon & Schuster Building,
Rockefeller Center,
1230 Avenue of the Americas,
New York, New York 10020
JULIAN MESSNER and colophon are
trademarks of Simon & Schuster.
Manufactured in the United States of America

10 9 8 7 6 5 4 3 2 1 (hardcover)

10 9 8 7 6 5 4 3 2   (paperback)

Design by Judith Hoffman Corwin

Library of Congress Cataloging-in-Publication Data

Corwin, Judith Hoffman.
  Jewish holiday fun.

  (Messner holiday library)
  Includes index.
  Summary: An activity book for celebrating Jewish
holidays by cooking, doing crafts, and learning things.
  1. Fasts and feasts—Judaism—Juvenille literature.
[1. Fasts and feasts—Judaism.   2. Jewish crafts.
3. Handicraft.   4. Cookery, Jewish.   5. Judaism—
Customs and practices] I. Title.   II. Series.
BM690.C67   1987   394.2′68296   86-18201
ISBN: 0-671-60230-6 (hardcover)
        0-671-60127-X (paperback)

Jewish Holiday Fun

א ב ג ד ה ו ז
ח ט י כ ל מ נ
ס ע פ צ ק ר ש ת

For Jules Arthur and Oliver Jamie and everybody
who loves a good celebration.

Messner Holiday Library
by Judith Hoffman Corwin

Birthday Fun

Christmas Fun

Cookie Fun

Easter Fun

Halloween Fun

Jewish Holiday Fun

Patriotic Fun

Thanksgiving Fun

Valentine Fun

Contents

For You

Jewish Holiday Fun tells about the legends and traditions of the Jewish people. Folklore, foods, and fun projects are included. Some of our modern-day foods, such as *challah*, honey cake and *hamantaschen* have their origins in events that took place long ago and are now celebrated by holidays. Ceremonial foods, such as the Passover *matzoh*, have deep meaning and they are described for each holiday. There is an explanation of the Jewish calendar and illustrations of the Hebrew alphabet. There is also a Noah's Ark, New Year's cards, Rebecca and Isaac paper dolls dressed in ancient ceremonial robes, Purim puppets, a *seder* plate, a *dreidel*, and an Israeli flag.

You will be able to make everything yourself, mostly using things you can find around the house.

Before You Begin

Make your own pattern

Directions for most of the projects in this book include patterns for you to make an exact copy of what is shown. You don't want to cut up the book, so make your patterns with tracing paper. First place a piece of tracing paper over the pattern to be transferred from the book. Using a pencil with soft lead, trace the outline of what is in the book. When you have finished, cut out what you have drawn on the tracing paper. Now you have your own pattern.

Using your pattern

Pin your pattern to the paper or fabric you have chosen to work with, or hold it down carefully. Draw around the edges of the pattern. Then lift up the tracing paper pattern and go on with the other instructions for your project.

Materials you will need

The basic materials you need are readily available from stationery stores and art supply shops: cardboard, oaktag, heavy white paper, and colored paper. Extras like cloth and bits of lace may be found at home or in fabric departments in stores. For details and accents, you'll need colored markers (waterproof), pencils, or watercolors and a paintbrush. You will also need a sharp pair of scissors and a good brand of white glue.

Preparing a work area

Before you begin to work, make sure all your supplies are at hand and that everything is neat and clean. Cover your work surface with newspaper to protect it from glue. (By the way, when you work with glue, always spread a thin, even coat. A thin coat sticks better and is less likely to cause the paper to buckle.)

For the cooking projects, you will need an adult to help you with the stove.

Most of the projects in **Jewish Holiday Fun** can be made quite easily. Some may prove to be more of a challenge, but you can do them all. Have fun!

"Clay" Recipe

Here is the basic recipe for the "clay" that is used for creating several projects in this book. It is used to make the moon pin and pendant for Rosh Hashanah, the fruits and leaves that hang from the Sukkah, the dreidel for Hanukkah and the seder plate for Passover. Each project made from the "clay" is completely different and an enjoyable addition to each holiday celebration.

MATERIALS:

tracing paper, cardboard
pencil, scissors, knife
acrylic paints, brushes
shellac, brush
permanent black, fine-line felt-tip marker

UTENSILS:

measuring cup
large bowl, spoon
cookie sheet
potholder

INGREDIENTS:

2 cups flour
1 cup salt
1 cup water

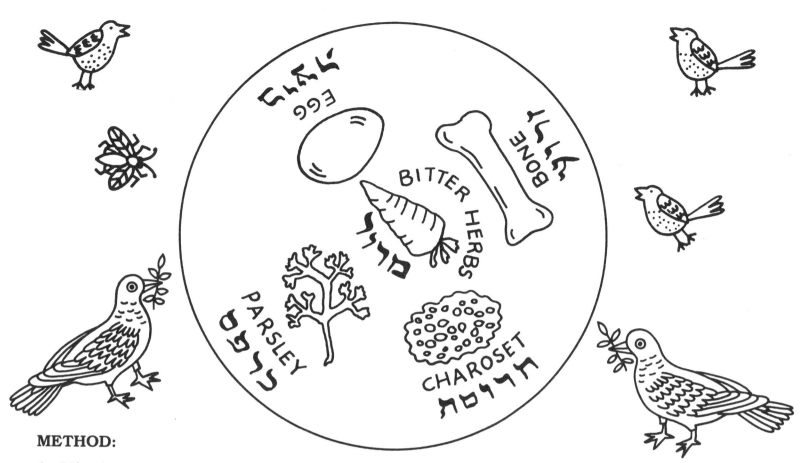

The seder plate shows (in Hebrew and English): EGG / ביצה, BONE / זרוע, BITTER HERBS / מרור, PARSLEY / כרפס, CHAROSET / חרוסת

METHOD:

1. Mix the flour and salt together in a large bowl. Add the water a little at a time, mixing it in. When all the water is used up, mix the dough well with your hands. This is called "kneading."

2. Continue to knead the dough until it is smooth.

3. Put some flour on a clean working surface and roll the dough to about 1/4" thick. (The dough will expand slightly when it is baked.)

4. Trace the patterns you want from the book and transfer them to the cardboard.

5. Place the cardboard cutout on the dough. Hold the cardboard down with one hand, then use your knife carefully to cut the dough around the pattern.

6. Set the oven to 300°. An adult should help you. Place the "clay" pieces on a cookie sheet at least 1" apart and bake until lightly browned. It takes about 30 minutes, but keep checking the oven to make sure that the pieces aren't burning along the edges.

7. Using a potholder to protect your hand, remove the cookie sheet from the oven. When the "clay" pieces are cool, take them off the cookie sheet.

8. Decorate with acrylic paints. See patterns for specific instructions. When they are dry, cover them completely with shellac to keep out any moisture and to preserve them.

TISHRI   HESHVAN   KISLEV   TEVET   SHEVAT   ADAR

12   NISAN   IYAR   SIVAN   TAMMUZ   AV   ELUL

Noah's Ark

The Noah's Ark toy was traditionally played with on days of rest, partly because it was special, but also because it took a while to set up all the different animals properly and enjoy them.

Included are Noah and his wife—Noah is pictured holding the book in which he enters all the animals that travel on his ark. These are the animals that you can make for your ark—two of each, because "the animals went into the ark two by two"—lions, tigers, elephants, horses, camels, reindeer, bears, alligators, birds, snakes, rabbits, squirrels, turtles, sheep, ducks, mice, dogs, cats, monkeys, fish, seal, chickens, frogs, and even butterflies and ladybugs.

MATERIALS:

1 large sheet of white oaktag
2 pieces of 15″ × 7″ cardboard
popsicle sticks or similar sticks from art
  supply shop
shoe box (preferably one with little or no
  printing on it) approximately 11¾″ ×
  6¾″ × 3½″

gray paint, paintbrush
tracing paper, carbon paper
pencil, tape, scissors
white glue
black fine-line felt-tip markers
felt-tip markers in assorted colors

METHOD:

1. The shoebox will be the ark itself and will also be used to store the finished animals. Paint the box, including the lid, with the gray paint. Set it aside to dry. If you like, you can put designs on top of the painted surface with the felt-tip markers. Check the illustration for design ideas.

2. The two pieces of 15″ × 7″ cardboard are to be the ark's roof. Glue them together along one 15″ side and tape them in place on the lid of the box to form the roof. The roof should center over the lid of the shoebox and overhang about 1¾″ on either side. You can also use tape to help to hold the roof in place while the glue is drying.

3. Now sketch in the windows, door and doves, checking the illustration for proper placement. Color in everything with the felt-tip markers.

4. To make Noah, his wife and the animals, begin by tracing the designs onto the tracing paper. Place a piece of carbon paper on top of the oaktag and tape it down gently. Tape the traced design on top of the carbon paper.

5. Draw over the design firmly with a pencil. Then remove the tracing paper and carbon paper. Draw over the outline of the design with the black, fine-line, felt-tip marker. Color in the design and then cut it out. Repeat for all of the designs. Remember to make two of each animal.

6. To make everything stand up, use a small piece of popsicle stick cut with the scissors. Follow the illustration. Secure with a small amount of glue to the reverse side of the piece. Now line up everybody in front of the ark and pretend that they are embarking on their great voyage!

18

19

21

24

Isaac and Rebecca Paper Dolls

Isaac and Rebecca are paper dolls dressed in ancient Jewish ceremonial costumes. Rebecca has two gowns complete with a headdress and a veil with the Star of David on it. Isaac has a robe decorated with beautiful embroidery and a shepherd's outfit. Best clothes are worn on the Sabbath, not the work clothes of the rest of the week.

MATERIALS:

oaktag (for dolls)
tracing paper
carbon paper
white paper (for doll's clothes)
bits of fabric and lace
small buttons
tiny beads
glue
scissors
pencil
felt-tip markers in bright colors
black fine-line felt-tip marker
tape

METHOD:

1. Place a sheet of tracing paper over the paper dolls and their clothes and trace them.

2. Place a sheet of carbon paper over the oaktag or paper. Place the tracing paper with the designs on it on top of the carbon paper.

3. Gently tape the three sheets together onto your working surface, at the top and bottom. This will prevent the papers from sliding around as you draw. Draw over the design on the tracing paper.

4. Remove the tracing and carbon papers. Draw over the designs with the black fine-line felt-tip marker. Cut them out. Color with the other markers. Bits of lace and fabric and a string of beads can be added as you wish.

26

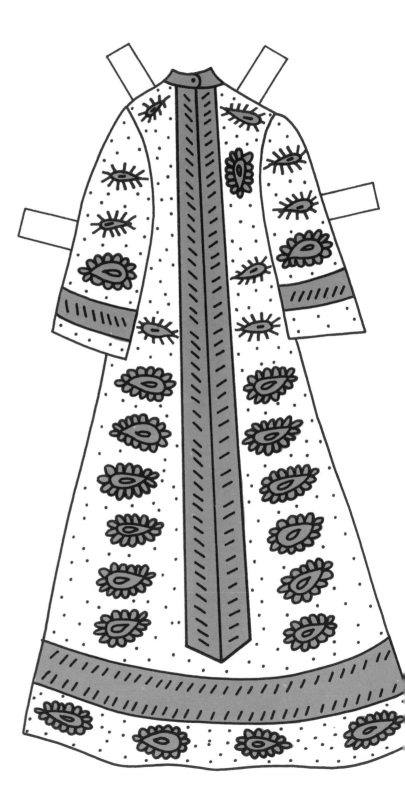

28

The High Holy Days: Rosh Hashanah and Yom Kippur

Rosh Hashanah and Yom Kippur are perhaps the most important Jewish holidays. They come in the fall when the Jewish New Year begins. *Rosh Hashanah* in fact means "beginning of the year" and is observed on the first and second days of the Jewish month of *Tishri. Yom Kippur,* which means "day of atonement," falls on the tenth day of Tishri. These holidays, unlike other Jewish holidays, are purely religious; they are connected neither with historical nor natural events. The High Holy Days are a time for thought and reflection as people look back upon how they have lived during the past year and recommit themselves to their ideals.

Rosh Hashanah begins in the evening with a holiday meal. *Challah,* the special bread for Jewish festive meals, is on the table, but this night, it is more likely to be round, instead of the usual ladder or braid shapes, to remind us that one year is over and a new one is beginning. The challah is dipped in honey so that the new year may be sweet. Fish is often served at this meal because fish symbolize fruitfulness and plenty.

The next morning, in the synagogue, the ram's horn or *shofar* is blown. In ancient times the shofar was blown at all important events.

More recently, the custom of exchanging New Year greeting cards has become very popular. These often contain the words *Shanah Tobah*—"a good year."

The first day of Rosh Hashanah starts a ten-day period of penitence and prayer that ends with Yom Kippur, the Day of Atonement. People who have done wrong are given ten days within which to repent. According to Jewish belief, on Rosh Hashanah the destiny of all mankind is recorded by God in the Book of Life, while on Yom Kippur what has been written is sealed and made final. If those who have sinned repent before Yom Kippur the judgment is changed and they are granted a good and happy New Year.

New Year's Cards

Exchanging *shanah tobah* greeting cards is a modern custom widely enjoyed. These lovely cards bring good wishes for a happy new year and are sent to relatives and friends. Designs are given for a lion and lamb, an olive tree with a dove, and showing the three biblical heroes of Israel: Samson, Bar Kochba and Judah Maccabee.

MATERIALS:

8½″ × 11″ white paper, 1 sheet for each card
tracing paper, carbon paper
pencil, scissors, tape
black fine-line felt-tip marker
colored felt-tip markers

METHOD:

1. To make each card you will need one sheet of paper folded so that it measures 5½″ × 8½″.
2. Choose the design you want to make and draw it on the tracing paper. You can make whichever one you like—or all of them!
3. Place a piece of carbon paper on top of the folded card and tape it down gently. Now tape the traced design on top of the carbon paper.
4. Draw over the design firmly with a pencil, then remove the tracing paper and carbon paper. Now draw over the outline of the design with the black felt-tip marker. Color in the design as you like.

Moon Pin and Pendant

The moon plays an important part in the celebration of the Jewish holidays. It is an invaluable measure of time. This funny pin and pendant are a charming way of remembering this. The pendant is a half-moon and the pin is a full moon, complete with a little man in the moon attached.

MATERIALS:

"clay" recipe
water glass with 3″ diameter, knife
toothpick
safety pin, tape
24″ piece of string
paint, paintbrush
shellac, brush

METHOD:

1. To make the pin and pendant, use the "clay" recipe on page 10. Roll out the "clay" and cut out two 3″ circles. You may use the glass to help you do this.

2. For the pendant, cut the moon's profile out of the circle, as shown. Also make a hole, as shown, with a toothpick before baking. Bake as directed, paint, shellac, and then insert the string through the hole. Secure the string with a knot and wear around your neck.

3. To make the pin, paint the moon's face, as in the illustration, and make a small man also from the "clay." He is easily formed from several small balls, as shown. Attach him to the side of the moon and bake as directed. Paint and shellac. Turn the finished moon to the reverse side and attach a safety pin with a piece of tape.

Sweet Honey Cake

Honey cake is traditionally served on Rosh Hashanah and is eaten from then until Simhat Torah. The Bible describes an ancient "sweet cake" that was a honey and jam cake.

INGREDIENTS:

3 tablespoons butter, softened
¾ cup dark brown sugar, firmly packed
3 eggs, slightly beaten
¾ cup honey
2¼ cups flour
¾ teaspoon double-acting baking powder
¾ teaspoon baking soda
2 teaspoons cinnamon
¾ cup cold coffee
½ cup chopped walnuts
½ cup orange marmalade
extra butter to grease the pan

UTENSILS:

large mixing bowl
measuring cups and spoons
rubber spatula
9 × 5 × 3 inch loaf pan
cooling rack, potholders
aluminum foil, plastic bag

DIRECTIONS:

1. Preheat the oven to 350°. Ask an adult to help you with this.
2. Stir the butter and brown sugar together in the large mixing bowl. Add the eggs and honey. Continue to stir the mixture until it is completely combined.
3. Beat in the flour, baking powder, baking soda and cinnamon. Add the coffee and mix well, scraping the bowl often with the rubber spatula. Stir in the walnuts and orange marmalade.
4. Grease the pan with the extra butter.
5. Pour the batter into the prepared pan. The batter will fill the pan almost to the top. After an hour of baking, check to see if the top of the cake is becoming too brown.

Cover the cake with aluminum foil, if necessary, to prevent it from burning before the cake is fully baked. Bake for about an hour, or until the top springs back when lightly touched.
6. Allow the cake to cool in the pan for 15 minutes before removing it to the cooling rack to cool completely. This cake is best eaten the next day because the honey flavor needs time to develop. Store it in a cool place in a tightly secured plastic bag.

34

Sukkot and Simhat Torah

Sukkot is the Hebrew word for "booths." The festival of Sukkot comes in the fall, shortly after the High Holy days. It lasts for nine days, from the fifteenth through the twenty-third day of the month of *Tishri*. For the first seven days Jewish people are to spend at least part of each day in small shelters or booths.

In this way Jews remember their ancestors and the days of wandering in the desert after the exodus from Egypt. These wanderers pitched tents or built booths wherever they stopped.

The *sukkah,* or booth, is built of wood or canvas and is covered with branches and plants in such a way that the heavens and the stars can be seen overhead. The inside of the sukkah is decorated with flowers, fruits and vegetables, and all meals are taken there. In most cases people go home to sleep.

The building and decorating of the sukkah is a happy time. Sukkot, coming as it does in fall, is also a festival of thanksgiving for the harvest. To give thanks for the bounty of the land Jews recite blessings over the etrog and the lulav. The *etrog* comes from the citron tree. It looks like a big lemon and is sharp but sweet at the same time. The *lulav* is made from the branches of the palm, myrtle, and willow trees.

The ninth day of Sukkot is now known as *Simhat Torah.* It is the day on which reading of the Torah is concluded and started over again.

For the Jews, the *Torah* is the most precious book. It contains the laws by which Jews live. It is written by hand with a feather pen on pieces of parchment made from sheepskin and rolled into a scroll.

The Torah is read throughout the year, a portion every week. By celebrating Simhat Torah we recognize that God's teachings are never to be forgotten. The Torah scrolls are carried around and around the synagogue in a long happy parade. There is much rejoicing and singing. Afterward refreshments are served; wine, cakes, candies, cookies and especially jelly apples—the sticky favorite of the children.

Build A Sukkah

Here's a chance to build your very own miniature sukkah. The center of the roof is left open to allow the sky to show through. Tiny fruits, vegetables and leaves are made to decorate it. There is even a little basket full of fall goodies resting near it.

MATERIALS:

8″ square of heavy cardboard, for the
  ground
7″ square of heavy cardboard, with a 5″
  square cut out from the center of it, for
  the roof
4 wooden dowels, 6″ long, for the sides of
  the sukkah
pencil, ruler, scissors
white glue, string
small twigs
green felt-tip marker
"clay" recipe

METHOD:

1. To make the roof of the sukkah, measure and draw a 5″ square in the center of the 7″ piece of cardboard. Cut out the 5″ square. Place the roof on a flat surface and glue the wooden dowels to each of the four corners. Allow to dry.

2. Put a little glue on the bottom of each of the wooden dowels and place the structure on the 8″ square of cardboard. Color in the ground and draw in blades of grass with the green felt-tip marker. Arrange the twigs on the roof of the sukkah.

3. To make the tiny fruits, vegetables, leaves and basket follow the recipe for the "clay" recipe on page 10. Take a small amount of the "clay" and form it into a ball. Then start to shape things more carefully, checking the illustration for ideas. Try making leaves, apples, lemons, pumpkins, squash, corn, clusters of grapes, peppers, carrots and eggplant. Bake everything as directed in the recipe. Color with acrylic paints, let dry and then shellac everything.

4. Glue some of the fruits, vegetables and leaves to the roof of the sukkah. Tie strings to others and hang them (secured by glue) to the roof and sides of the sukkah. Place the basket on the ground, next to the sukkah, and arrange other leaves and vegetables around it.

Autumn Apples

Autumn is the true apple season and these beautiful ones will add a tasty treat to your Sukkot celebration.

INGREDIENTS:

5 medium-size McIntosh apples
2/3 cup light corn syrup
2 cups sugar
1 cup water
a few drops of red food coloring

UTENSILS:

5 popsicle sticks
medium-size saucepan with cover
large mixing spoon
candy thermometer
paper towel
aluminum foil

DIRECTIONS:

1. Wash the apples and insert a popsicle stick in each one. Set aside to dry on a paper towel.
2. Combine the corn syrup, sugar and water in the saucepan. Stir the mixture and bring it to a boil. Cover the saucepan and cook for about 3 minutes more.
3. Uncover the saucepan and continue to cook until the surface of the mixture has a cracked appearance. On the candy thermometer this should read 290°.
4. Add the red food coloring and quickly dip each apple in the mixture. Place them upside down on a sheet of aluminum foil. Enjoy your harvest!

Hanukkah

Hanukkah, which takes place from the twenty-fifth day of *Kislev* to the second day of *Tevet*, is also called the Festival of Lights. It is one of the happiest of Jewish holidays.

Over two thousand years ago, the Syrians and Greeks took the Temple in Jerusalem away from the Jews. They filled the Temple with statues of their gods and tried to force the Jews to worship these idols. The Jews refused and were treated very harshly by their conquerors. A small group of Jews, under Judah Maccabee, decided to fight for their freedom. Maccabee means "hammer," and for three years these soldiers, known as the Maccabees, hammered at the enemy until, at last, Jerusalem was freed. When the Maccabees reentered the Temple, they found that the lamp of Eternal Light was no longer burning. Though they searched and searched for the special oil with which to relight the lamp, only a tiny jar—enough for one day—could be found. A miracle occurred, however. The oil lasted for eight days, during which time the Jews celebrated the rededication of the Temple. *Hanukkah* means "dedication," and now we know why it is also called The Festival of Lights. Since that time, the eight days starting with the twenty-fifth day of *Kislev* are kept as a joyous festival in memory of the rededication of the Temple.

Today Hanukkah is celebrated by lighting the *Menorah,* a Hanukkah lamp with places for nine candles, eight for the eight days during which the miraculous oil burned, and a ninth with which to light the others. Using the extra candle or *shammash,* we light candles every night, starting with one and adding to it each day, until on the eighth day all eight candles are lit.

Unlike other Jewish holidays, there is no special feast for Hanukkah. There is much merrymaking and exchanging of gifts. A favorite treat to serve at this time is the *latke,* or potato pancake. In some places it is the custom to prepare a meal of dairy foods in which different cheeses are served. A favorite Hanukkah game is the spinning of the *dreidel,* a top with four sides.

Dreidel

The *dreidel* is used to play a Hanukkah game. It is spun like a top for pennies, nuts, or candies. The goodies are put on the floor near where the game is to be played. The dreidel has four sides, each with a Hebrew letter on it. They are *nun, gimmel, hay* and *shin*. Everyone has a turn to spin the dreidel. If it lands on *nun*, you don't get anything. If it lands on *gimmel*, you will win all the goodies. When the dreidel lands on *hay*, you are entitled to half of the goodies. Finally, if it lands on *shin*, you will have to give back some of your winnings.

MATERIALS:

"clay" recipe
blue acrylic paint
paintbrush
black fine-line felt-tip marker
shellac, brush

שׁ ה ג נ

METHOD:

1. To make the three-dimensional dreidel, use the "clay" recipe on page 10. Follow the illustrations for the size and overall shape. Begin by making a 4″ ball from the dough. The bottom of the dreidel must come to a point and the top should be narrow enough to be easily held. Refine the shape by checking the illustration.

2. Bake it as directed. Allow it to cool and then paint it with a coat of light blue acrylic. Dry, and then with a permanent black fine-line felt-tip marker draw each letter on the proper side of the dreidel. Also draw in the designs and paint them in with bright colors. Shellac the dreidel, let it dry, and begin playing!

Hanukkah Cookies

These delicious cookies can be made for Hanukkah or any other festive Jewish holiday, except Passover. Several favorite holiday symbols are used as patterns to make these cookies from. Patterns are given for a candle, the Star of David, a dreidel, the moon, and a dove.

INGREDIENTS:

1 cup sweet butter, softened
8 ounce package cream cheese
¾ cup sugar
2 teaspoons vanilla
3½ cups flour
extra flour to roll out the dough
extra vegetable shortening to grease the
   cookie sheets

UTENSILS:

large-size mixing bowl
measuring cups and spoons
large wooden spoon
rolling pin
cookie sheets
potholder

MATERIALS:

tracing paper
oaktag
pencil
scissors

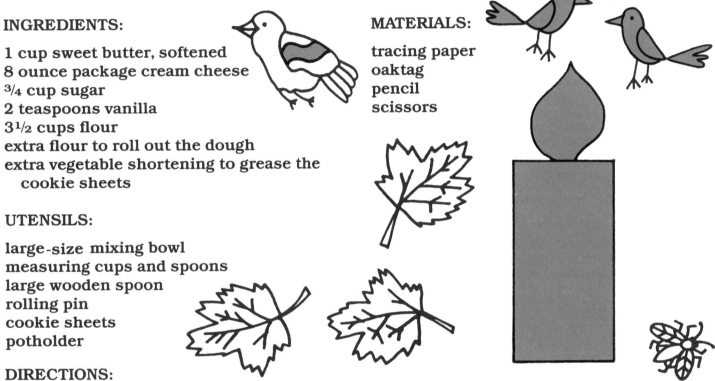

DIRECTIONS:

1. Stir the butter in the large mixing bowl until it is light and fluffy. Beat in the cream cheese, a little at a time.
2. Add the sugar and vanilla. Add the flour and continue to stir the mixture until it is completely combined. You will now have a nice stiff dough to work with.
3. Roll the dough into ¼″ thickness on a lightly floured surface.
4. Preheat the oven to 350°. Ask an adult to help you with this.

5. Trace the patterns for all the designs on the tracing paper. Put the tracing paper on top of the oaktag and hold together with one hand. With the other hand, cut all around the outside edge. Repeat this for all of the designs until you have an oaktag pattern for each of them.
6. Place the cardboard pattern on the rolled-out dough. Again hold it in place with one hand and cut all around the outside edge with a knife. Lift the pattern and re-

peat for all of the designs. Make as many cookies of each design as you like.

7. After the cookies have been cut out with the patterns, place them one inch apart on lightly greased cookie sheets.

8. Bake for 10–15 minutes, or until lightly browned. Allow to cool.

9. Ice with either the chocolate icing, colored icing, or prepared icing that comes in tubes. The prepared icing can be bought in the supermarket in a variety of colors. Another super-simple way of decorating these cookies is to spread sifted confectioners' sugar over them. Just put the cooled cookies onto a large sheet of waxed paper and sift a little of the sugar over each cookie to give it a gentle "dusting."

Yield: about 24 cookies.

Colored Icing

INGREDIENTS:

2 egg whites
1/2 teaspoon cream of tartar
3 cups sifted confectioners' sugar
red, yellow, blue and green food coloring, a
   few drops of each

UTENSILS:

medium-size bowl
egg beater
5 small bowls
toothpick
paper towels

DIRECTIONS:

1. In a medium bowl, beat the egg whites and the cream of tartar with the egg beater until very foamy.

2. Beat in the confectioners' sugar gradually, until the icing stands in firm peaks and is stiff.

3. Divide the icing among five small bowls; leave one plain (white); tint the remaining with food coloring. Using the toothpick, ice the cookies. To keep the icing from drying out while you are working with it, cover the bowls with damp paper toweling. Store any leftover icing in tightly covered jars in the refrigerator. Makes about 1 1/4 cups of icing.

Note: Eyes can be made with raisins or small candies. This is if you aren't going to "paint" them on with the colored icing. Chocolate sprinkles, colored sugars, chopped nuts, silver dragees, cinnamon red-hots, or small chocolate-covered candies can also be used to decorate the cookies. These should be put onto the cookies before they are baked.

41

43

Tu bi-Shevat (Arbor Day)

Jews have a special new year—for trees. Trees are especially important to Jews because they are a symbol of life, and in a desert country like Israel they are life itself.

The new year for trees falls on the fifteenth day of the Jewish month of *Shevat*. It is a time when the first green buds are appearing and the sap begins to rise. It is a time for rejoicing and looking forward to the coming of spring.

The holiday has its origins in the Torah, which forbade the eating of the fruit of a tree during its first three years. On the fourth year the fruit is given as a gift to God and from the fifth year it may be eaten by all. By giving trees a "birthday," it is easier to keep track of how old they are and to obey this law.

Although *Tu bi-Shevat* is not mentioned in the Bible and there are no laws for its observance, it is still a very special day.

Even when the Jews were driven from the land of Israel and lived in cold climates where trees did not bloom at this time of year, they still kept this day. On this day Jews throughout the world remembered the beauty of the Holy Land and celebrated the holiday by eating the fruits that grew there, such as grapes, raisins, almonds, dates, and figs. They also ate the special fruit of the carob tree.

Today, Jews outside of Israel celebrate Tu bi-Shevat with special attention to the state of Israel, its geography and its products, and by buying certificates for the planting of trees in Israel. Millions of trees have been planted in this way.

In Israel itself the festival is of great importance. For years the land of Israel was bare of trees and shrubs—a desert. One of the most important tasks of the new settlers was to turn the desert green, and on this day the children in Israel are given the privilege of planting new trees so that the land shall live and thrive.

Tree Mobile

A soft spring breeze will make these simple felt trees dance. The mobile is great fun to watch; even at night the shadows will be wonderful.

MATERIALS:

2 squares of green felt
wire hanger
scissors
green thread, needle

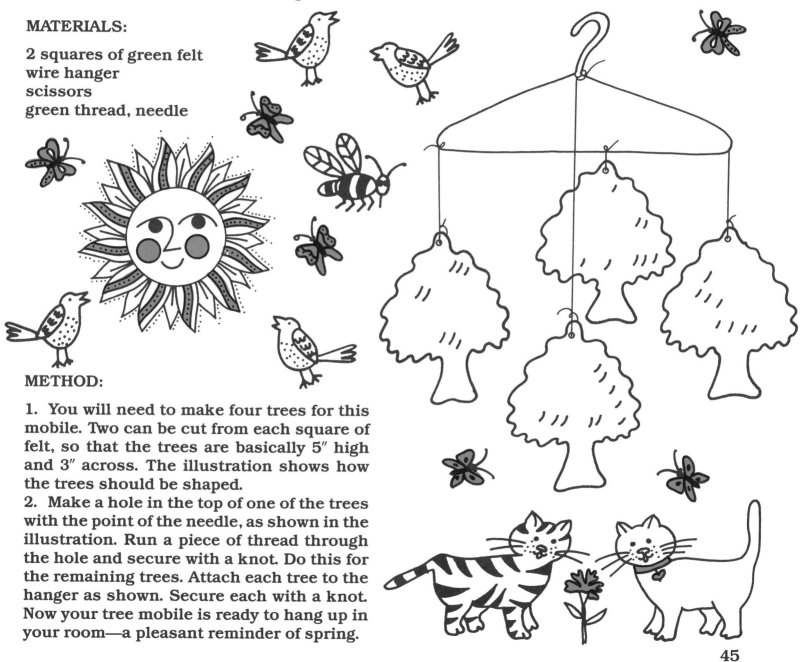

METHOD:

1. You will need to make four trees for this mobile. Two can be cut from each square of felt, so that the trees are basically 5″ high and 3″ across. The illustration shows how the trees should be shaped.

2. Make a hole in the top of one of the trees with the point of the needle, as shown in the illustration. Run a piece of thread through the hole and secure with a knot. Do this for the remaining trees. Attach each tree to the hanger as shown. Secure each with a knot. Now your tree mobile is ready to hang up in your room—a pleasant reminder of spring.

45

Purim

Purim is a happy day, a day for rejoicing with the first breath of springtime. It takes place on the fourteenth and fifteenth days of the Jewish month of *Adar*, and it celebrates the story of Esther and Mordecai, long ago in the land of Persia.

A king of ancient Persia was named Ahasuerus; his young and beautiful queen was named Esther. The king did not know that his beloved queen was Jewish.

One day, Esther's cousin, Mordecai, overheard two soldiers plotting to kill the king. Mordecai quickly told Esther, who informed the king. The story of how the king's life was saved was entered into the palace records.

The king's chief adviser was named Haman. He was a wicked and vain man who expected everyone to bow down when he walked through the streets. Mordecai would not bow before Haman, since a Jew bows only to God. Haman determined to kill not only Mordecai, but every Jew in Persia! To decide on the most favorable day for the slaughter, Haman cast lots, or *purim*, from which the holiday gets its name.

Haman had convinced the king to go along with his plan. But the king learned of Mordecai's part in saving his life and had also listened to the pleas of Esther. She had first fasted for three days to pray for guidance and strength, and then told him that if he were to kill all the Jews, then she must die too since she was Jewish.

The king had the wicked Haman hanged, spared the Jews, and made Mordecai his chief adviser.

Ever since, Jews have observed Purim. The day before Purim is a day of fasting, in memory of Esther's fast. The fast is followed by two days of dancing, merrymaking, feasting and gladness.

One of the highlights of Purim is the feast which features *hamantaschen*, three-cornered cakes filled with poppy-seeds, apricots, or chopped prunes and raisins; these remind us of the triangular cap Haman is said to have worn.

46

The *Megillah* is the scroll on which the Book of Esther—the story of Purim—is written. The Megillah is read in the evening as the first stars appear.

Synagogues are mostly solemn places, but on Purim the atmosphere changes as children rattle *gragers*, or noisemakers, at every mention of Haman's name. Purim merrymaking also includes *Purim spielers*, boys and girls dressed up as the characters in the Purim story as they act out, once again, the great events.

The giving of charity *(shaloah manot)* is another highlight of Purim; even the poorest person is obliged to give at least one gift to two other people. These often consist of food that may be eaten without further preparation, such as boiled meat, candy, fruit, or wine. What better way to remember this day of Purim!

Purim Paper Puppets

The beautifully decorated puppets are made of the four famous Purim characters: King Ahasuerus, Queen Esther, Mordecai, her cousin and Haman, the king's chief adviser.

MATERIALS:

tracing paper, carbon paper
1 sheet of white oaktag
pencil, scissors, tape
black fine-line felt-tip marker
colored felt-tip markers
white glue
4 strips of heavy cardboard (12″ × 1″)

METHOD:

1. Draw the design for a puppet onto the tracing paper.
2. Place a piece of carbon paper on top of the oaktag and tape it down gently. Tape the traced design on top of the carbon paper.
3. Draw over the design firmly with a pencil. Remove the tracing paper and carbon paper. Draw over the outline of the design with the black felt-tip marker. Color in the design as you like. Repeat this for the other three puppets.
4. Turn the puppets to the reverse side and glue a strip of heavy cardboard to each. These cardboard strips should be placed at the top of each puppet's head, so that the extra length will extend beyond the puppet's body. This will allow you to hold and move them freely.

48

49

51

Hamantaschen

Hamantaschen, a Purim sweet or cookie, is named for Haman's three-cornered hat. Some people say it represents Abraham, Isaac and Jacob, who helped to save the Jews.

INGREDIENTS:

1 stick of sweet butter, softened
2 tablespoons confectioners' sugar
2 egg yolks
3 tablespoons ice water
1½ cups flour
apricot jam
butter to grease the cookie sheet
flour to roll the dough on

UTENSILS:

large mixing bowls
measuring cups and spoons
spatula, knife
rolling pin
plastic wrap
cookie sheet, potholders
water glass with 2″ diameter

DIRECTIONS:

1. Cream the butter and sugar together in the large bowl. Add the egg yolks and continue to mix well.
2. Add the ice water. Gradually stir in flour until a ball of dough is formed. Place the dough in plastic wrap and refrigerate it for several hours or overnight.
3. Turn on the oven to 350°. Ask an adult for help. Grease the cookie sheet with the extra butter.
4. It will be easier to handle the dough if you divide it in half and leave one half wrapped in the plastic in the refrigerator. Roll out the dough on a clean, lightly floured surface to a ¼″ thickness. Cut it into 2″ circles. You can use the top of a glass to "press out" the circles if you like. Fill each hamantaschen with 1 teaspoon of the jam and fold into three-cornered cookies: start by pressing two sides together, then

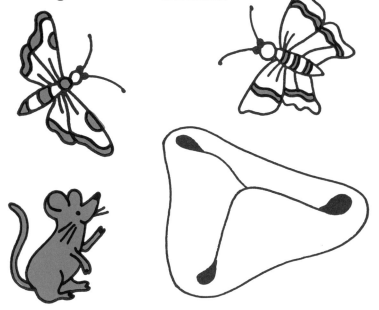

fold the third side over and press the ends together.
5. Place the hamantaschen about an inch apart on the greased cookie sheet and bake for 10–15 minutes, or until lightly browned along the edges.
Makes about 12 hamantaschen.

53

Passover

Passover, *Pesach* in Hebrew, which begins on the fifteenth day of the Jewish month of *Nisan* and lasts for eight days, is the Jewish festival of freedom. On Passover the deliverance of the Jews from slavery in Egypt is remembered.

When the Jews first settled in Egypt they were welcomed and prospered. But later, they were made slaves and lived in misery.

Everyone remembers the story of Moses and how he was saved from the river by the daughter of Pharaoh. The name Moses means "drew him out of the water." Although Moses was raised as the grandson of Pharaoh, when he grew up God told him to go to Pharaoh and say, "Let my people go." When Pharaoh refused, God punished Egypt with ten plagues: The rivers turned to blood, frogs covered the land, insects swarmed over the people, cattle died, and the people were made to suffer boils, hail, locusts and darkness.

The last plague was the death of the firstborn sons. On this night Jews marked their doorposts with the blood of a sacrificed lamb, so that the Angel of Death would *pass over* their houses and spare their firstborn sons. It was then that the Jews were told to leave Egypt. They left in such a hurry that they did not have time to bake the next day's bread. They did not even have time to leaven the dough to let it rise.

By the time the Jews reached the Red Sea, Pharaoh had changed his mind and sent his army to bring them back to slavery. By a miracle, the waters parted, letting the Jews cross. When the soldiers followed, they were swallowed up and drowned. The Jews were saved and free at last.

This festival of freedom and escape from slavery is celebrated at home as a family feast of remembrance called the *Seder.* The telling of the tale of freedom is known as the *Haggadah,* the Hebrew word for telling. The Seder is always conducted in the same order—*seder* is the Hebrew word for "order."

The seder table has a special seder plate with five symbolic foods: a roasted lamb bone; a green herb (parsley); bitter herbs (horseradish); a mixture of chopped nuts, apples and wine; and a roasted egg.

The lamb bone is for the sacrificial lamb; the bitter herbs because it was bitter to be a slave; the mixture is for the clay the Jews used to make Pharaoh's bricks; the egg is for the regular offerings in the Temple and greens are for the fruits of the earth. *Matzoh,* or unleavened bread, is served to remind us of the first night of flight.

Guests are often invited to the Passover seder, and as the seder begins it is said, "Let all who are hungry come and eat."

Making Matzoh

When we eat matzoh it serves to link us to the ancient story of Passover.

Matzoh is made from only flour and water, using no rising agent—yeast or other leavening. The matzoh that is used for the Passover seder is made under strict laws. Special flour is needed and the whole process of making it—the mixing, kneading, piercing and baking—must take eighteen minutes or less. The reason is that if it took more time the bread might rise and therefore not be appropriate for the seder. The recipe that follows is fun to make and quite easy, but should not be used for the seder.

INGREDIENTS:

3 cups flour
1½ cups water
extra flour to knead the dough

UTENSILS:

large mixing bowl
measuring cups
rolling pin, fork
cookie sheet

DIRECTIONS:

1. Turn on the oven to 450°. Ask an adult for help.
2. Put the flour in a large mixing bowl and gradually add the water. Begin to knead the dough with your hands, adding extra flour if necessary, until you get a pliable mound of dough. This should take 3–5 minutes.
3. Divide the dough into eight balls; roll each of these into a circle and make into a piece of matzoh.
4. Using a fork, make rows of holes in each of the matzohs in a neat pattern. Place the matzoh on the cookie sheet and bake for about 10–15 minutes, or until lightly browned. Makes 8 matzoh.

Seder Plate

Here's how to make a seder plate that is decorated with the *Pesach*, or Passover, symbols. It is divided into five different sections: one each for a lamb bone (shank bone), a green herb (parsley), a roasted egg, bitter herbs (horseradish), and one for a mixture of chopped nuts, apples and raisins (charoset). You can put the actual food on top of the designs on the plate if you like.

MATERIALS:

"clay" recipe
8″ cake plate
rolling pin, knife
white acrylic paint, paintbrush
permanent black fine-line felt-tip marker
colored acrylic paints
shellac; brush

METHOD:

1. To make the seder plate use the "clay" recipe on page 10.
2. Roll out the dough to ¼″ thickness. Place a small 8″ plate on top of the dough and use it as a pattern to cut the dough out.
3. Bake the plate as directed and then paint it with white acrylic paint.
4. Checking the illustration, sketch in the designs on the plate. Draw the designs large enough to fill the plate. With the black felt-tip marker go over the designs and the names of the foods. "Color in" the seder plate with the acrylic paints and then shellac it.

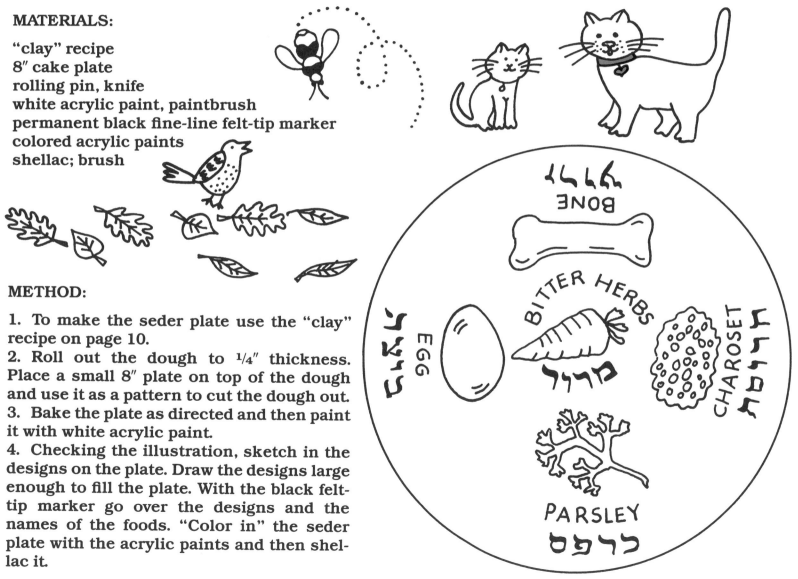

57

Shavuot

Shavuot is celebrated on the sixth and seventh days of the Jewish month of *Sivan*; this is at the end of spring. The name of the holiday is the Hebrew word for "weeks" because Shavuot comes exactly seven weeks after the second day of Passover.

In ancient times Shavuot marked the harvest of the wheat. Loaves of bread were baked of flour from the new wheat and were brought to the Temple at Jerusalem as thanksgiving offerings. The first fruit was also gathered at this time and brought to the Temple.

Shavuot is important for another reason: on this day God revealed himself to Moses on the top of Mount Sinai, and it was there that Moses received God's teaching, the Ten Commandments.

Holiday food for Shavuot includes dairy food, cheesecake, and blintzes (pancakes stuffed with cheese). It is customary to cover the floors with greens and to decorate the house and synagogue with plants and flowers.

In the synagogue an important part of the service is the reading of the Ten Commandments. Another part of the service is the reading of the Book of Ruth. The story of Ruth takes place in the fields during the harvest and is about a young girl who decides to give up worshipping idols to become a Jew. Ruth was the great-grandmother of King David.

Since Shavuot honors the time when the Jews received the law of God, in recent years it has also become the occasion to honor boys and girls who have studied in Hebrew or Sunday Schools. At the completion of their education, usually around the age of 15, they are confirmed in their faith in a special part of the Shavuot service at the synagogue.

Crepe Paper Flowers

Flowers always add a festive touch to any celebration and these are very colorful and super-simple to make.

MATERIALS:

rolls of crepe paper in yellow, orange, blue, red and green
package of pipe cleaners
scissors, stapler
white glue
small vase or glass

METHOD:

1. Cut a 15″ piece of crepe paper to make each flower. Roll it up tightly and insert a pipe cleaner to make the stem. Secure the flower by fixing one staple on either side of the pipe cleaner. Gently shape the crepe paper to make it look fuller and more flowerlike.

2. Cut out two leaves for each flower from the green crepe paper. With a tiny drop of glue, attach them to the pipe cleaner right under the flower.

3. Make about a dozen flowers and arrange them in the vase.

Israel Independence Day

The tiny State of Israel holds a special, very important place in the heart of every Jew. For thousands of years the Jews were a people without a homeland, living in the far corners of the earth, often persecuted and miserable, prevented from freely practicing their religion.

They thought often of the land of their forefathers, the Holy Land, the land of the Bible, and many a Jewish celebration was accompanied by the toast and hope: "Next year in Jerusalem."

The rebirth of the Jewish homeland occurred on May 14, 1948. It was declared in Tel-Aviv that "we . . . hereby proclaim the establishment of the Jewish State in Palestine, to be called Israel." That wonderful event is now celebrated as Israel's Independence day, on the fifth day of *Iyar*, with parades and joyous celebration in Israel and in many Jewish communities all over the world. The symbol of these celebrations is the flag of Israel. The flag is white with two blue stripes (white and blue are the colors of the Jewish prayer shawl). In the center is the ancient *Mogen David*—the Star of David. The flag was first used in 1897, and in 1948 it was adopted by the State of Israel.

Israel Independence day is a time to remember the long history of the Jewish people and their struggle against hardship and persecution. It is a time to recall the struggle of the young state of Israel to maintain its independence and security. It is a time to recall with pride the accomplishments of the Jewish people and those of the State of Israel, where the desert has been made to bloom.

It is a time to pray and hope for an end to war and suffering so that all the peoples of the world may live together in peace.

MEDITERRANEAN SEA

LEBANON

SYRIA

Haifa
Nazareth

West
Bank

Tel Aviv

JORDAN

Gaza
Strip

Jerusalem

Dead Sea

ISRAEL

Negev

Sinai

EGYPT

Elat

SAUDI ARABIA

The Flag of Israel

The flag of the modern state of Israel is the symbol not only of that young country, but of the entire Jewish people. It combines the design of the Jewish prayer shawl with the six-pointed Star of David, long a symbol of the Jews. The blue and white colors are also said to stand for the sky and purity.

MATERIALS:

1 yard white muslin
light blue, medium-width felt-tip marker
pencil, ruler
scissors, tape
brown wrapping paper

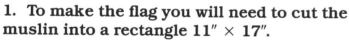

METHOD:

1. To make the flag you will need to cut the muslin into a rectangle 11″ × 17″.
2. Prepare your working surface by placing a sheet of brown wrapping paper, larger than your piece of muslin, on your worktable. Tape the piece of muslin that is to be your flag to the wrapping paper by placing a small piece of tape on each of the corners. If you have to color in these areas you can touch them up after you have finished coloring in the rest of your flag.
3. Sketch in the Star of David lightly on the muslin with the pencil. The Star is made by overlapping two triangles. You might want to draw in the stripes with a ruler. Check the illustration for proper placement.
4. Color in the Star and the stripes with the blue felt-tip marker.

63

Index